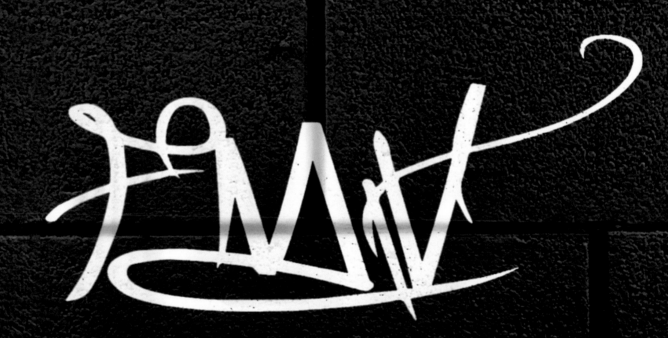

FEEL MY VISION

MARQUEL PARTEE

To order additional copies of this book, contact:
Xlibris
844-714-8691
www.Xlibris.com
Orders@Xlibris.com

ISBN: Softcover   978-1-6641-8761-0
        Hardcover   978-1-6641-8762-7
        EBook   978-1-6641-8760-3

Print information available on the last page

Rev. date: 07/29/2021

Feel My Vision

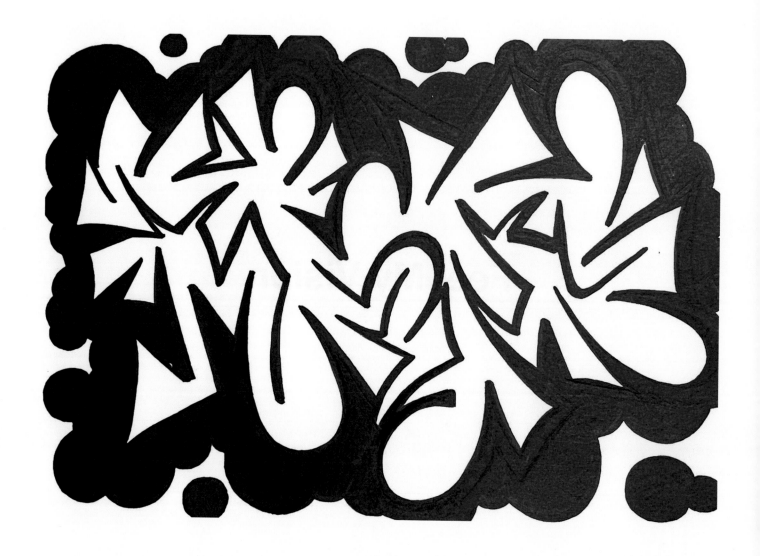

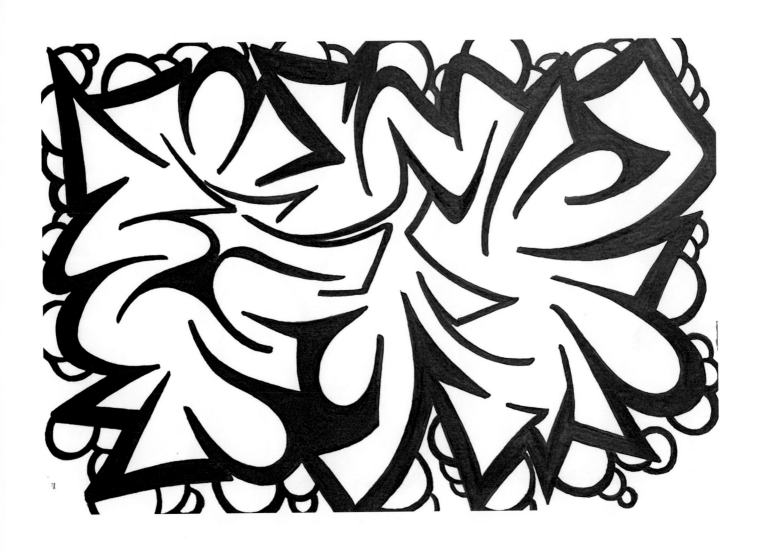

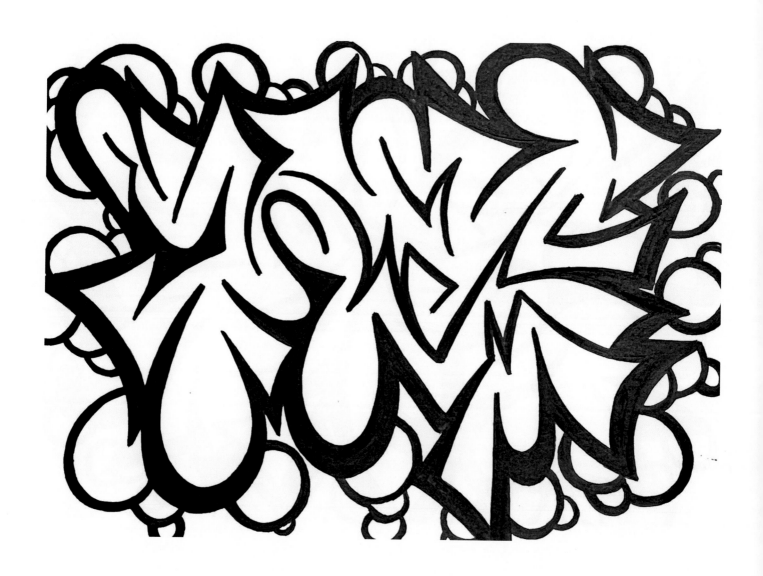

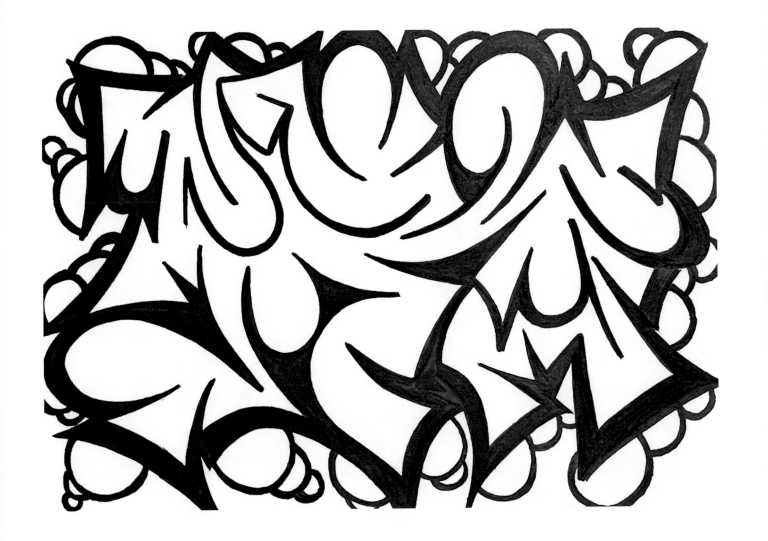

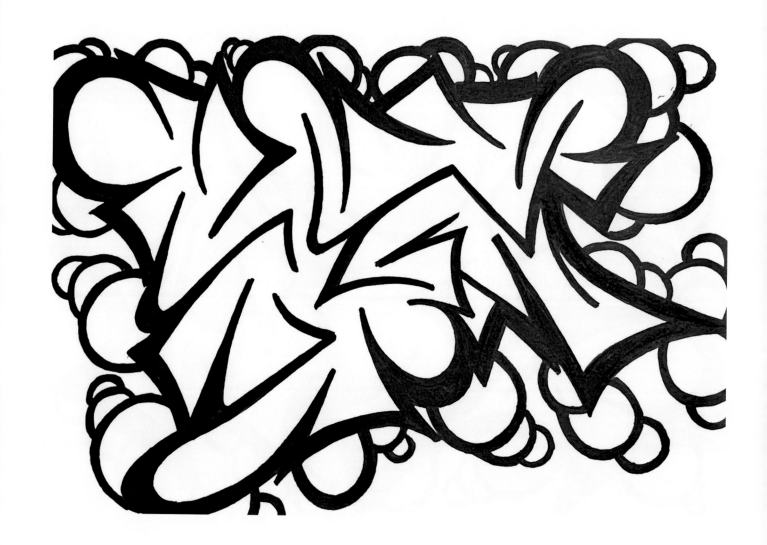

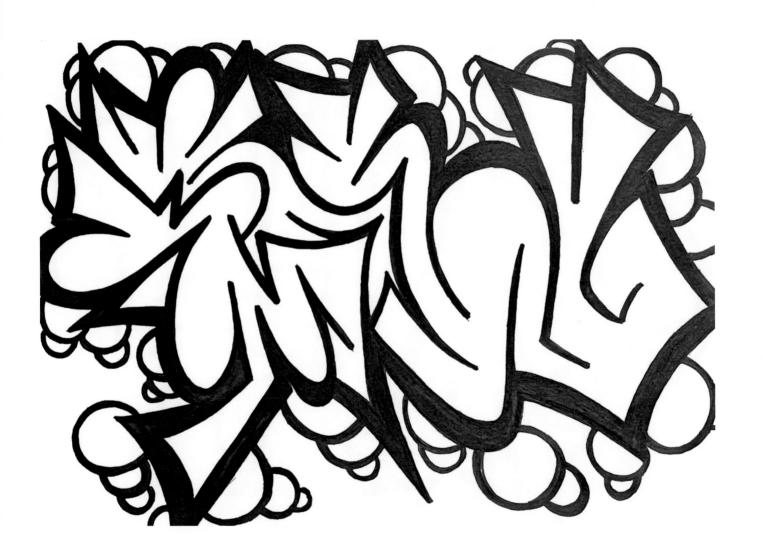

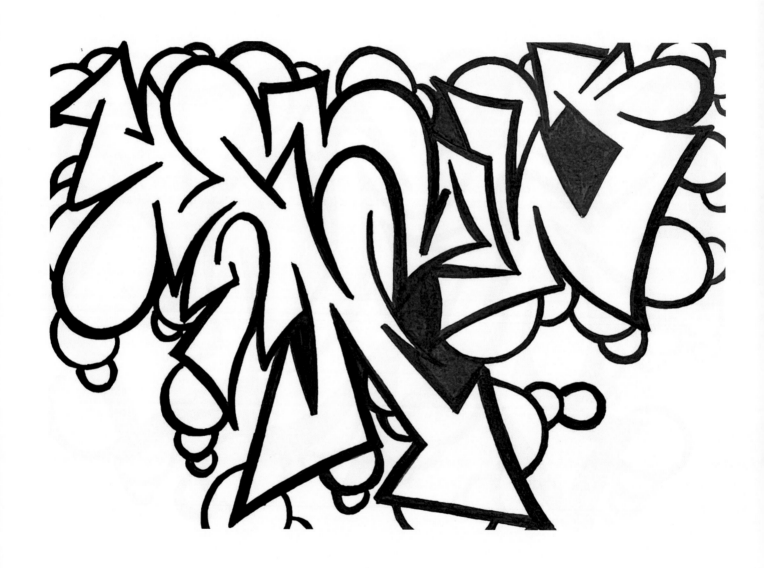

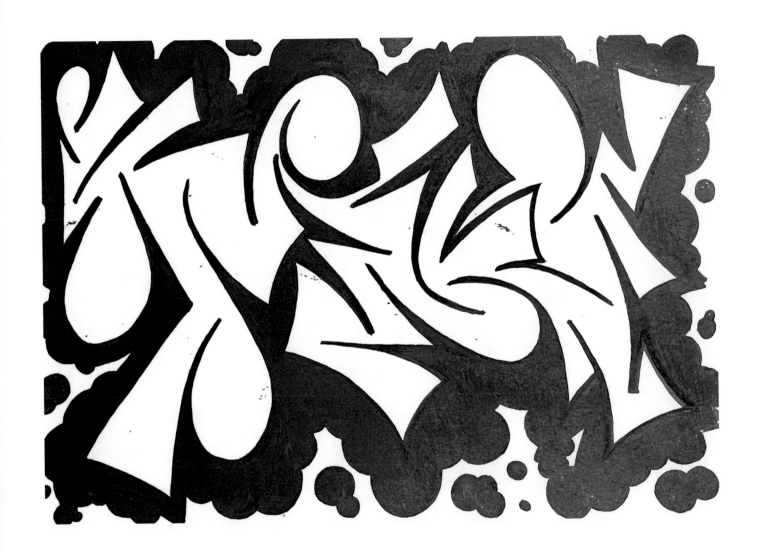

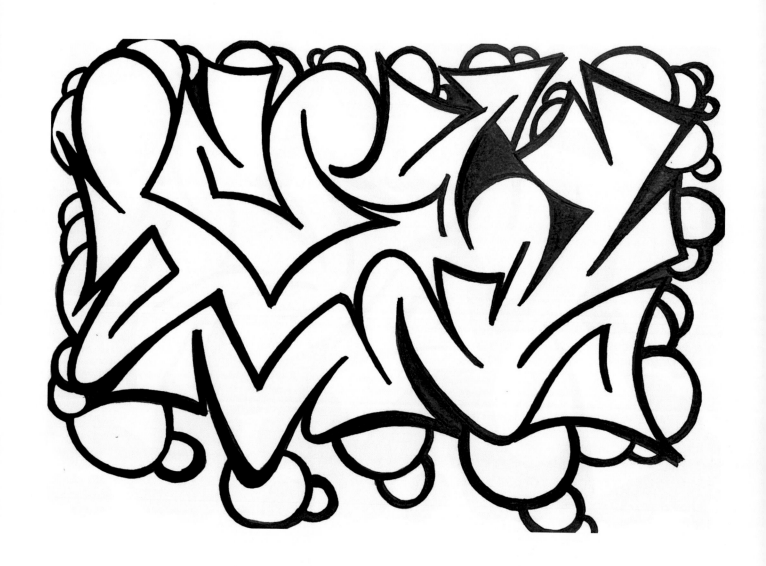

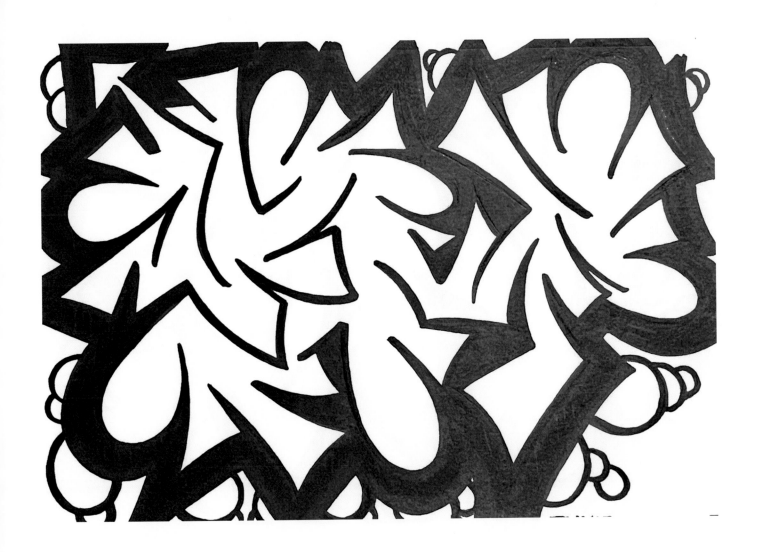

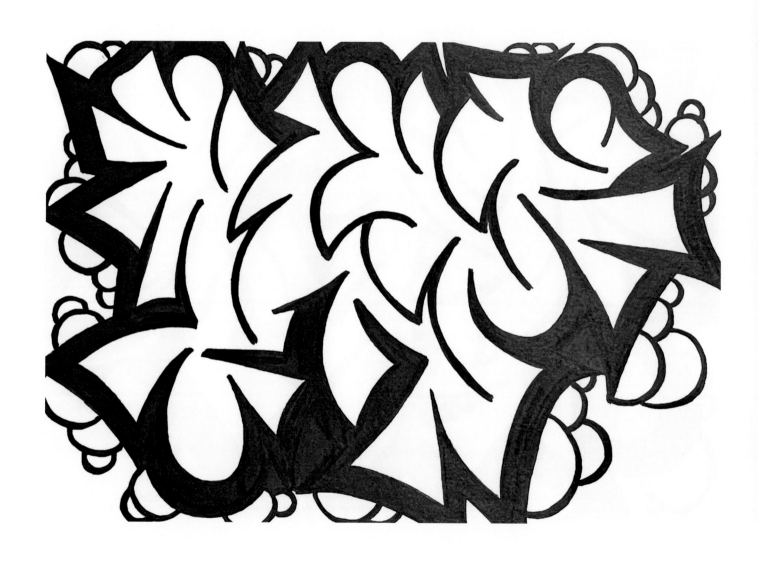

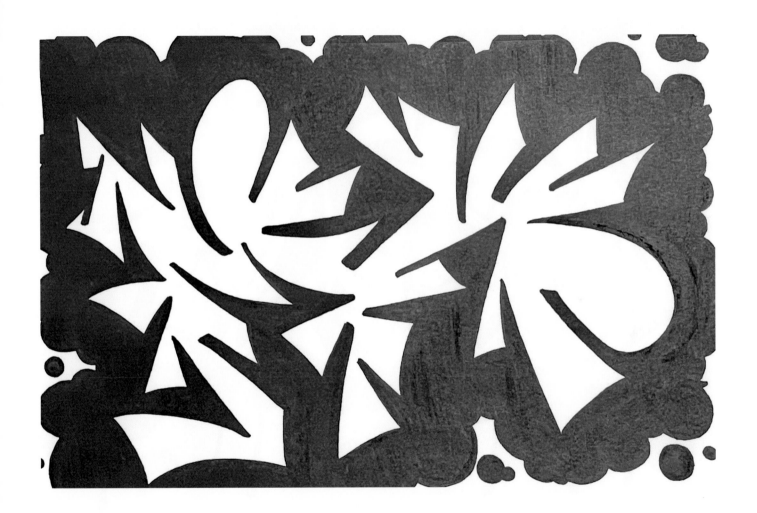

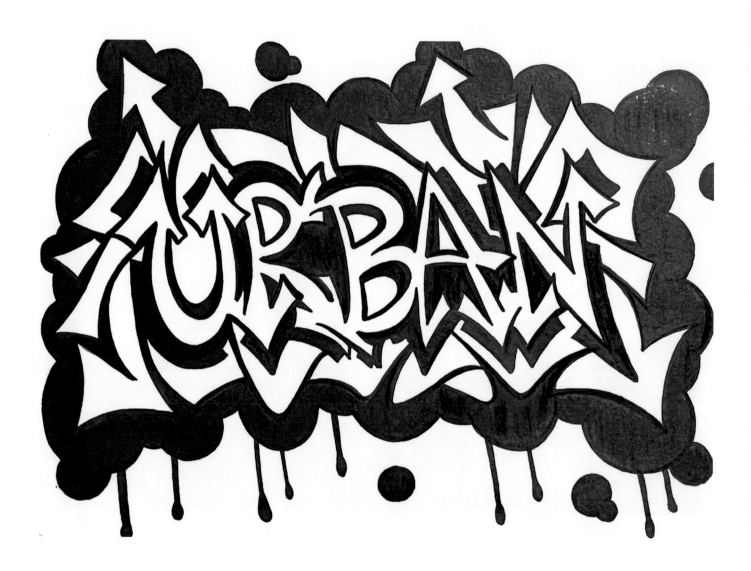

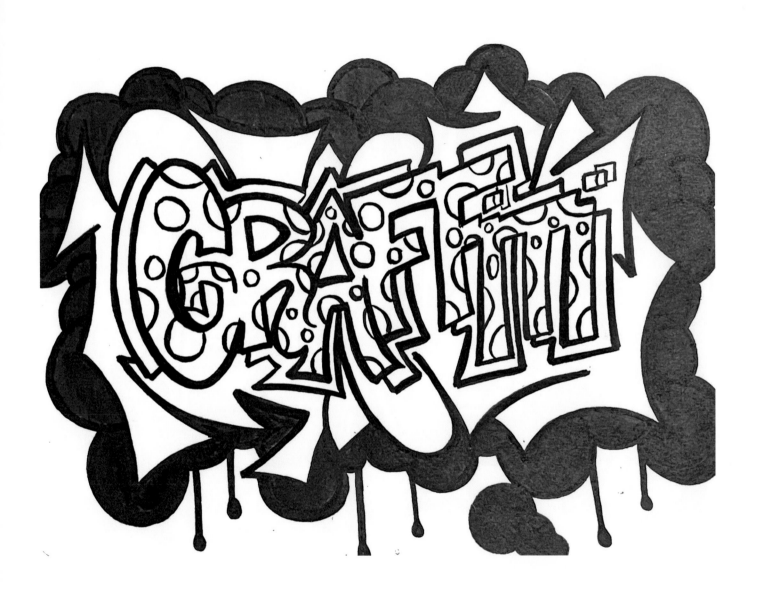

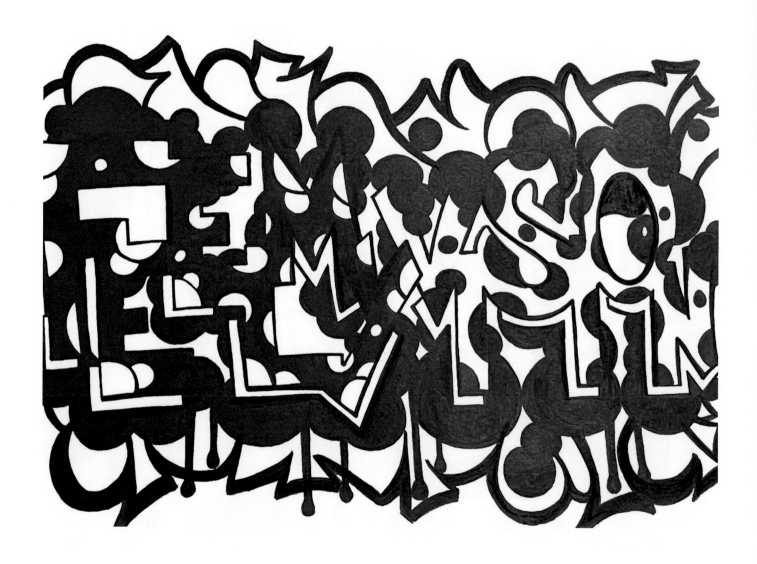

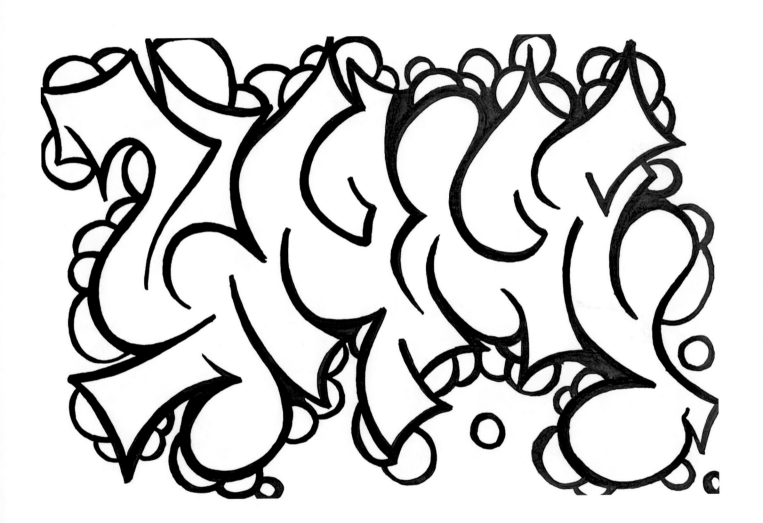

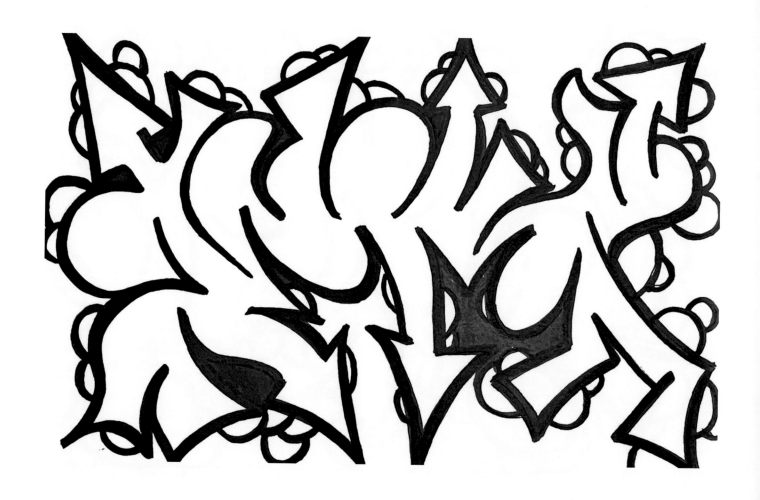

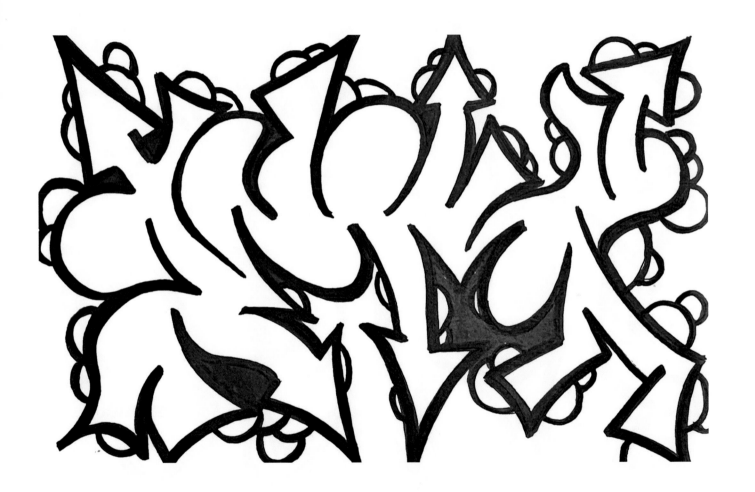

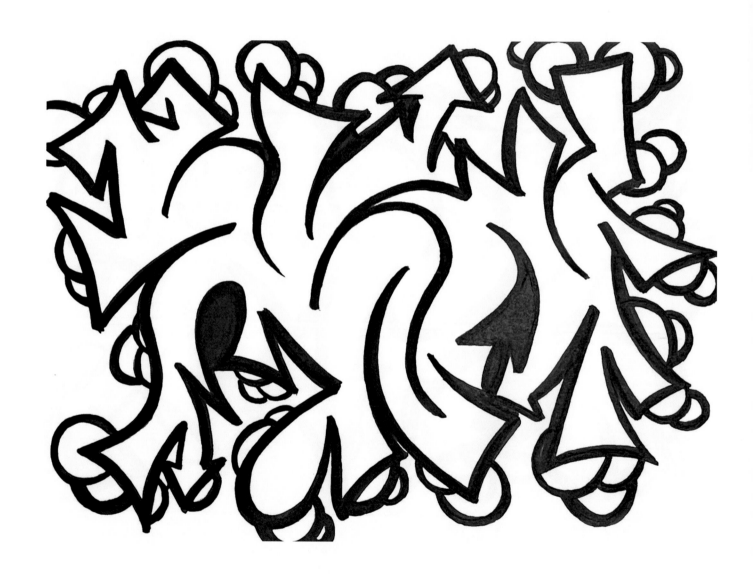

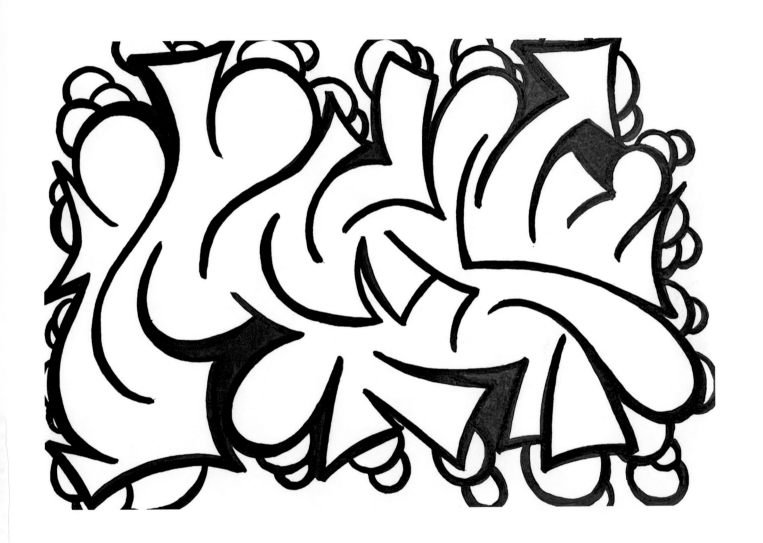

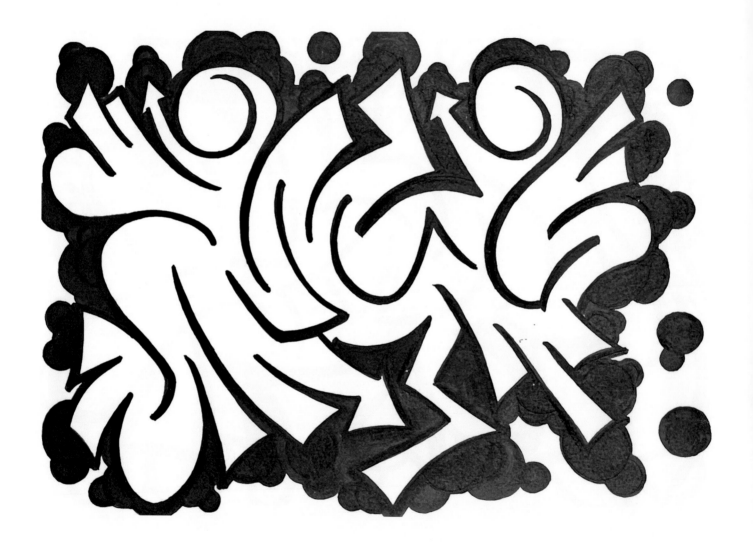

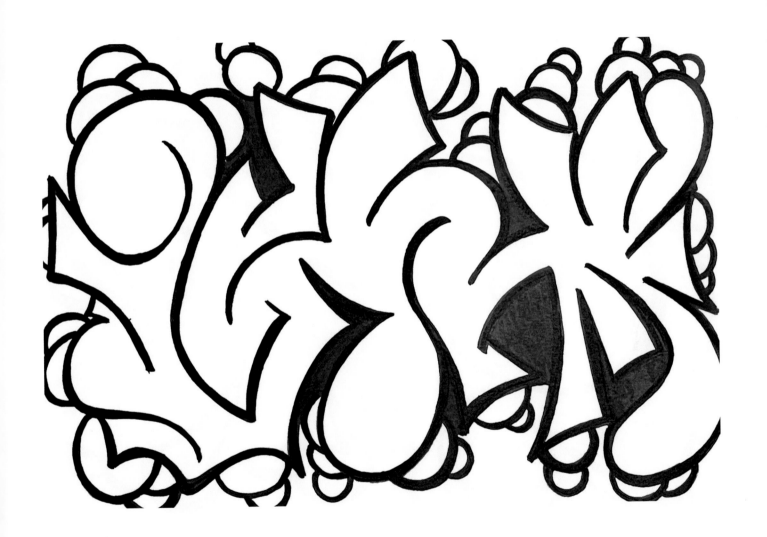

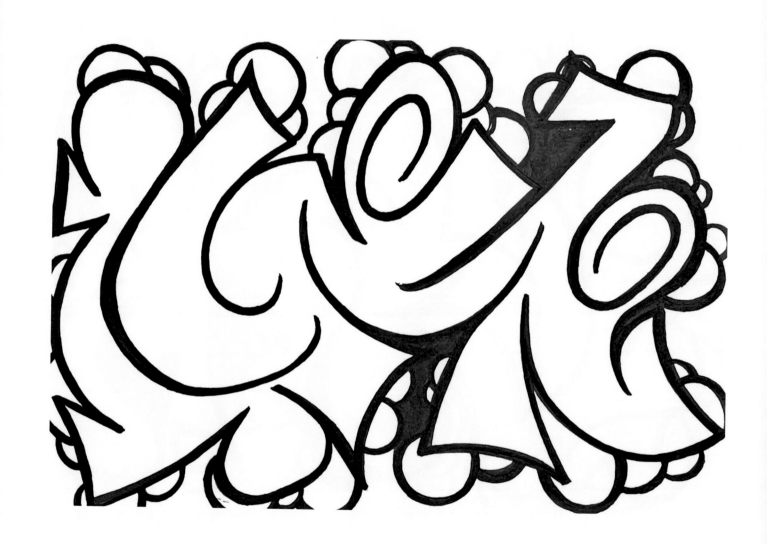

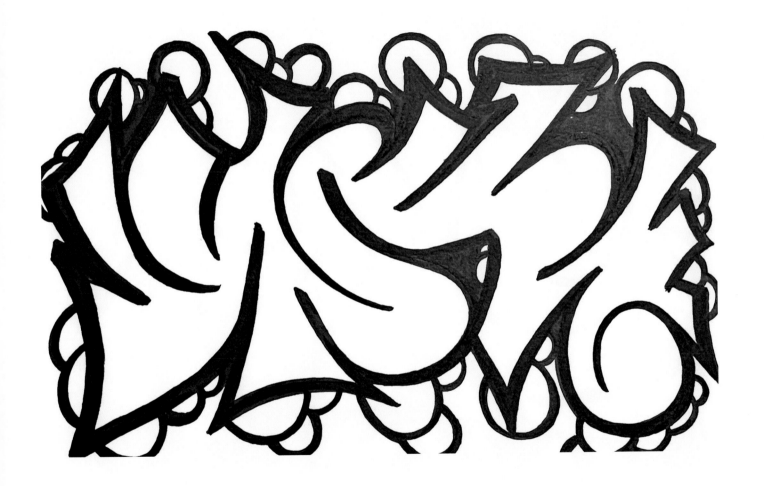

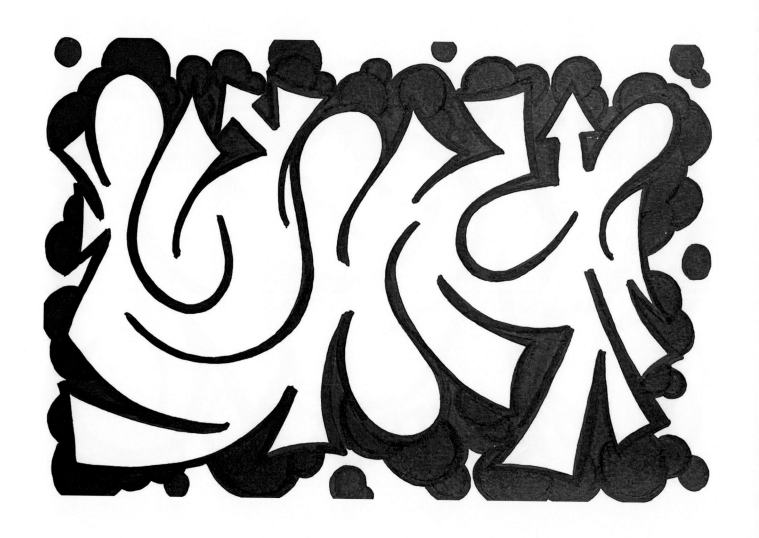

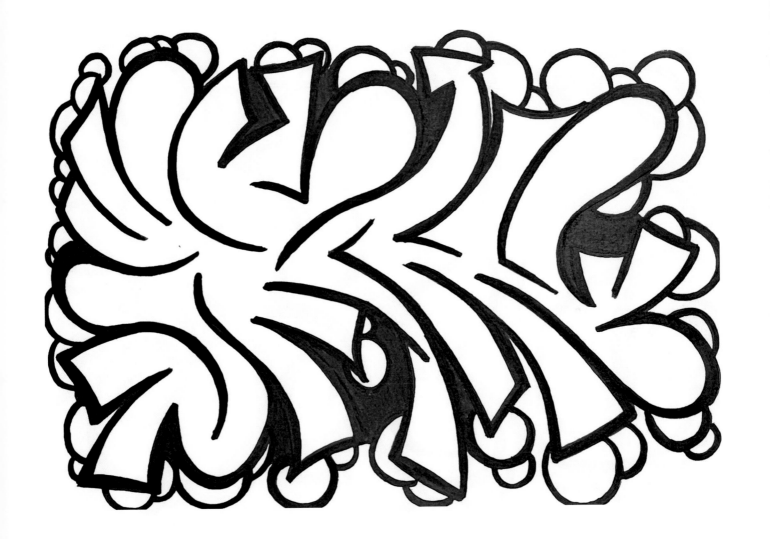

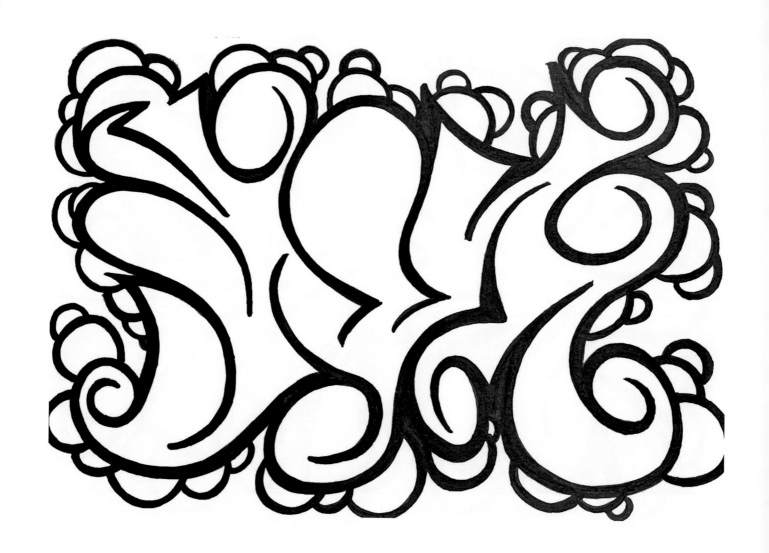

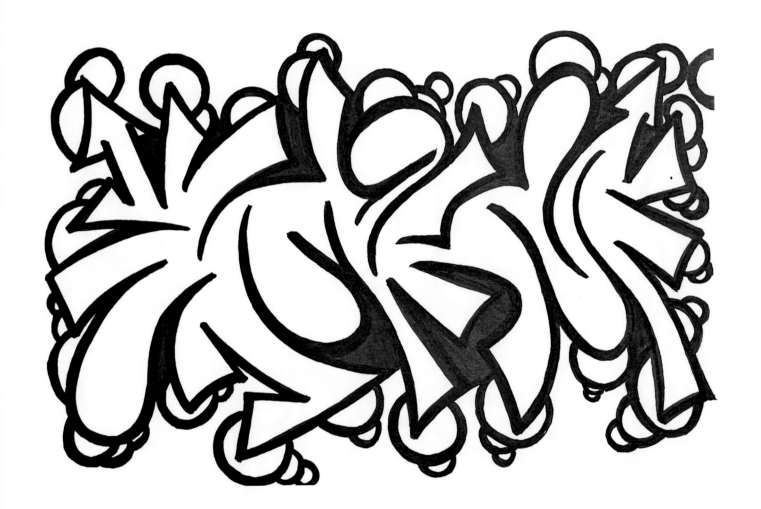

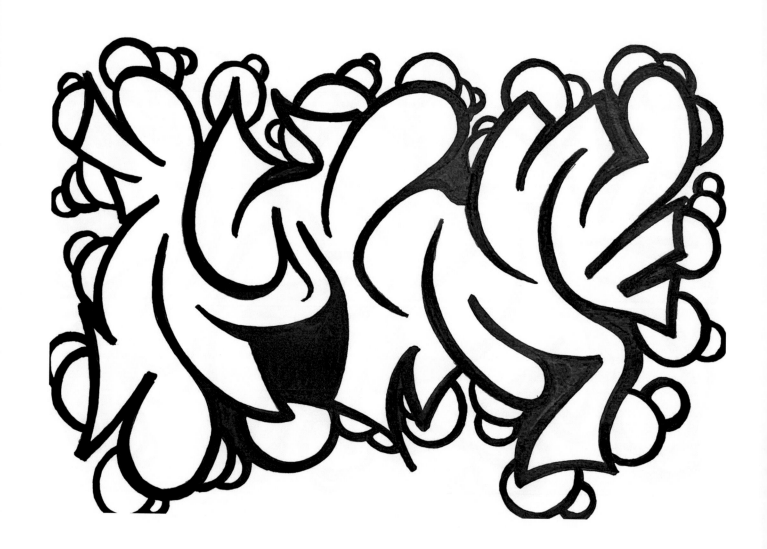

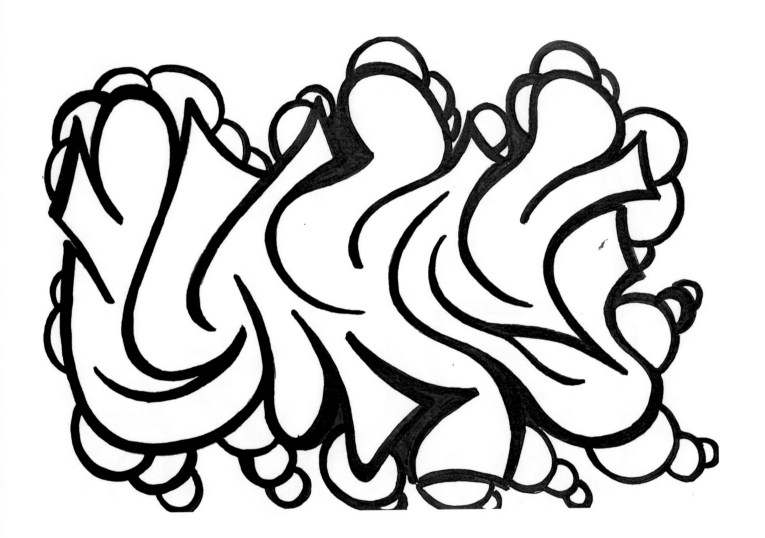

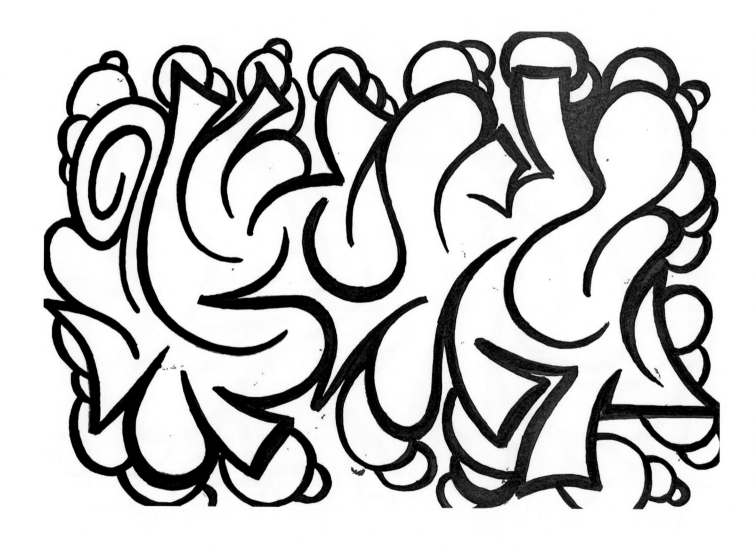

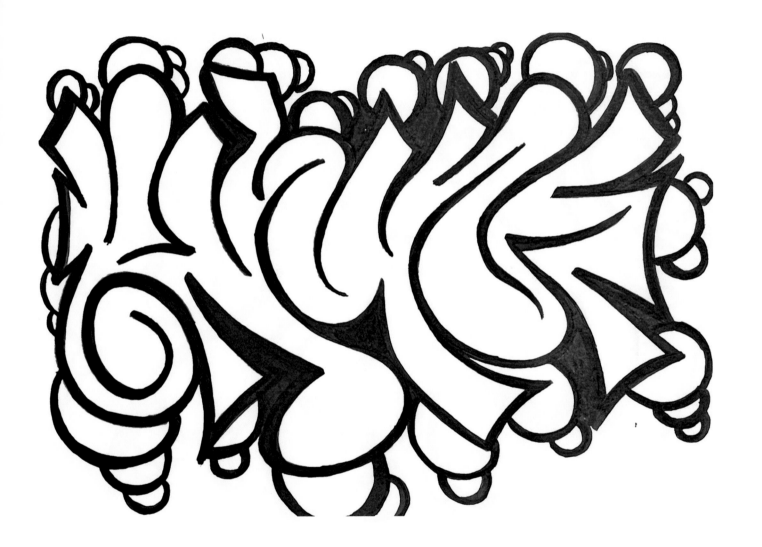

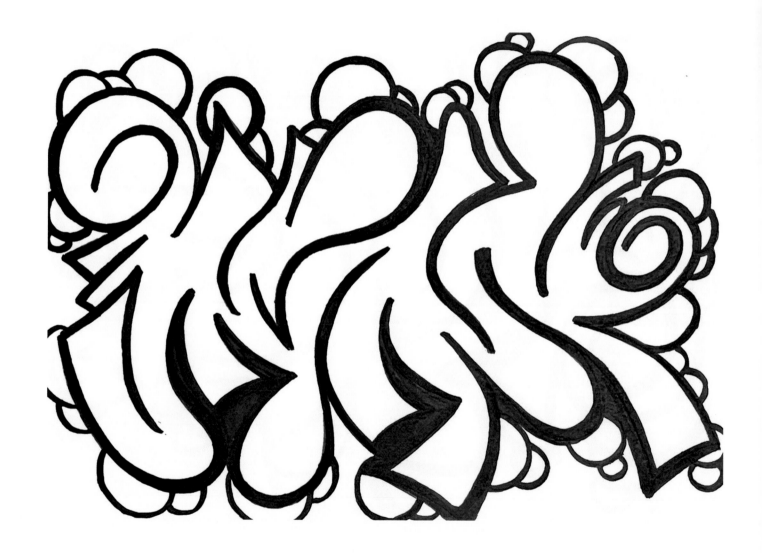

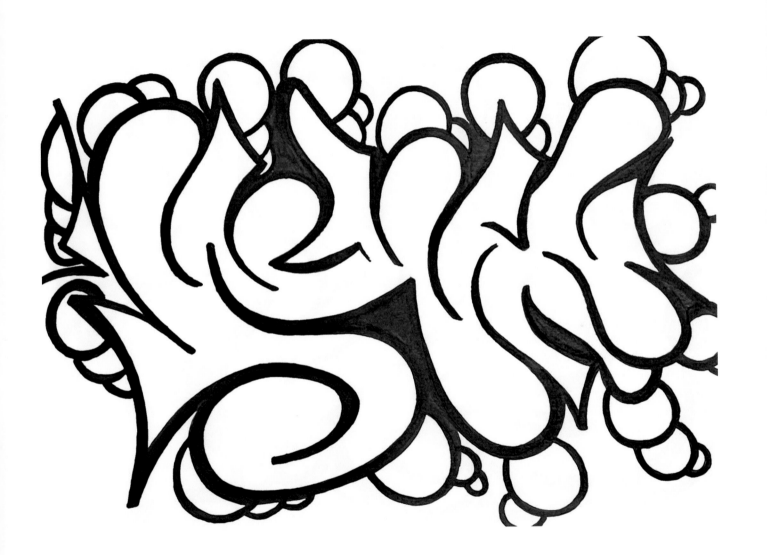

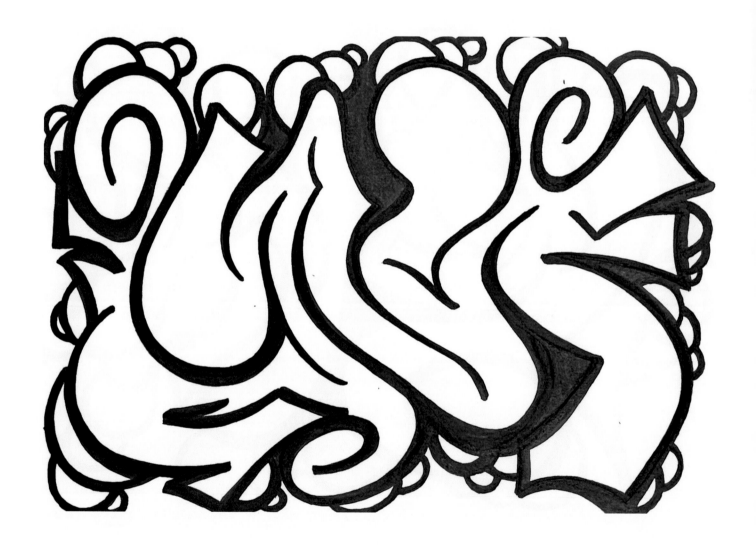

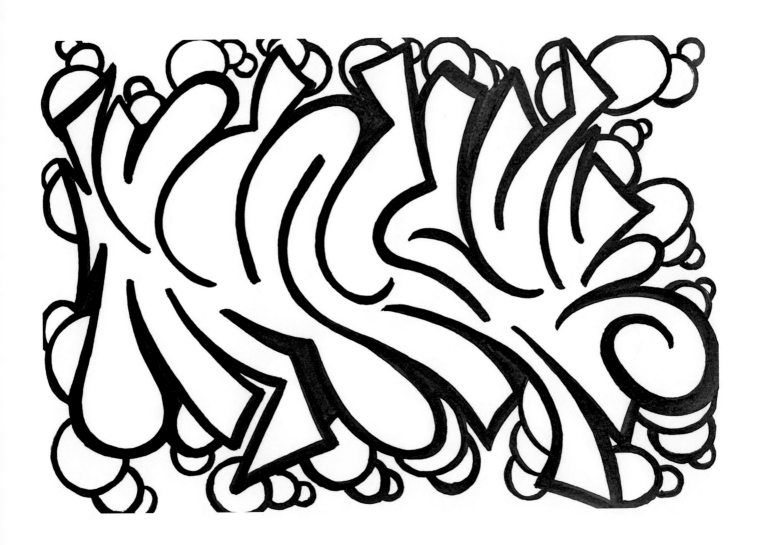

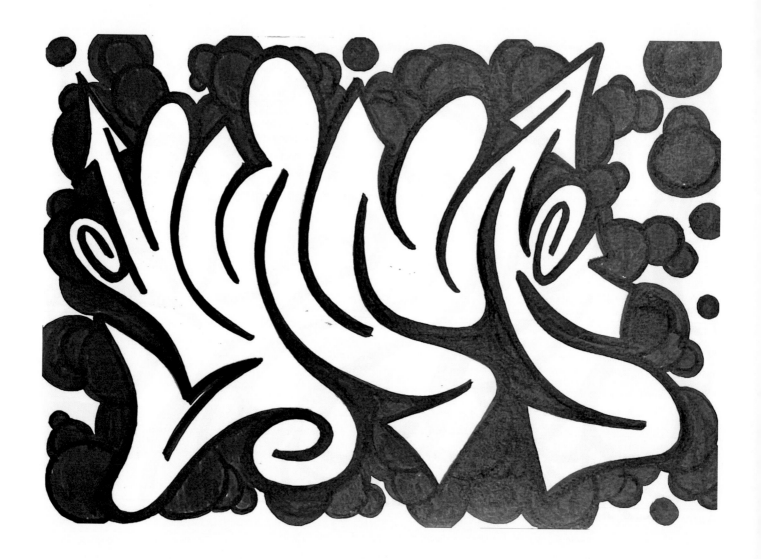

Printed in the United States
by Baker & Taylor Publisher Services